What Was Reconstruction?

by Sherri L. Smith

illustrated by Tim Foley

Penguin Workshop

This book is dedicated to all of the builders
of a better, more just tomorrow—SLS

PENGUIN WORKSHOP
An imprint of Penguin Random House LLC, New York

First published in the United States of America by Penguin Workshop,
an imprint of Penguin Random House LLC, New York, 2022

Copyright © 2022 by Penguin Random House LLC

Penguin supports copyright. Copyright fuels creativity, encourages diverse voices,
promotes free speech, and creates a vibrant culture. Thank you for buying an authorized
edition of this book and for complying with copyright laws by not reproducing, scanning,
or distributing any part of it in any form without permission. You are supporting
writers and allowing Penguin to continue to publish books for every reader.

PENGUIN is a registered trademark and PENGUIN WORKSHOP is
a trademark of Penguin Books Ltd. WHO HQ & Design is a registered
trademark of Penguin Random House LLC.

Visit us online at penguinrandomhouse.com.

Library of Congress Control Number: 2022031121

Printed in the United States of America

ISBN 9780593225936 (paperback)   10 9 8 7 6 5 4 WOR
ISBN 9780593225943 (library binding)   10 9 8 7 6 5 4 3 2 1 WOR

Contents

What Was Reconstruction? 1

The End of Slavery 6

Lincoln's Plan 11

A Blaze of Glory 21

New President, New Plan 35

The Same Old South 48

The First Americans 56

The Fight for Freedom 60

Radical Reconstruction 70

The Rise of Redemption 83

Dark Days 91

Legacy 100

Timelines 106

Bibliography 108

What Was Reconstruction?

In the early hours of May 13, 1862, a military steamboat made its way past the guards at Fort Sumter outside of Charleston, South Carolina. The United States was in the middle of the Civil War. The Northern states were fighting against the South over slavery. The North wanted slavery to end, but the South was determined to keep it. Eleven Southern states had broken away and formed a new country—the Confederate States of America. South Carolina was a Confederate state.

The soldiers at Fort Sumter thought the steamboat passing by was on their side of the war. But they were wrong. The man at the wheel was *not* a Confederate officer on routine business. His name was Robert Smalls. He was an enslaved

Robert Smalls

African American who had been forced to work on the ship. Every day he worried his family would be sold away from him. But now he was making an escape!

The white captain had left the steamboat to spend the night with his family. As on other nights, Smalls and some other enslaved crewmen invited their own families to visit them onboard. But tonight, instead of leaving, the women and children hid. And now, in the early hours, they were all steaming north to freedom!

"Although born a slave," Smalls later said, "I always felt that I was a man and ought to be free, and I would be free or die."

A few hours later, Smalls's steamboat reached

the Union ships guarding the coast. There, he offered his ship, and later his service, to continue the fight against slavery.

Smalls could not have imagined how much his life was going to change. He went on to meet President Abraham Lincoln, the man who helped bring an end to slavery. He served in the Union army. When the war ended, Smalls and his family returned to South Carolina. In 1874, he was elected to Congress. He was among the first African Americans to serve in federal government.

But the most unexpected change may have come after Smalls learned that the stately house of his former enslaver was for sale. Smalls bought it! He lived the rest of his life in the house where he had once been considered property. This huge reversal of fortune was thanks to the tumultuous period of change in post–Civil War America known as Reconstruction.

Reconstruction is the name for the post-war recovery that took place from 1865 to 1877. Black people became citizens and got the right to vote. Over these twelve years, the nation would attempt to rebuild itself in a new image. Many Americans hoped to see a stronger, fairer country emerge. But what began as a time of hope also proved to be a time of terror and sorrow, especially for the nation's newest citizens, African Americans.

CHAPTER 1
The End of Slavery

For more than two hundred years, wealthy white farmers in the South depended on enslaved Africans to work in their fields and wait on them

as servants. They considered enslaved people to be property, not human beings.

In 1861, a new president, Abraham Lincoln, took office. He was from Illinois. Like other Northern states, Illinois had abolished, or ended, slavery. The South feared that President Lincoln was going to outlaw slavery everywhere, something the South would not stand for.

CONFEDERATE STATES OF AMERICA

So eleven states seceded, or withdrew, from the Union. They banded together to create a separate country called the Confederate States of America. It was also known as the Confederacy.

Did the Southern states have the right to do this? President Lincoln and his allies said they did not. And so the Northern army went to war to defeat the Confederacy and bring all the Southern states back into the Union.

President Lincoln soon realized freeing enslaved people was the key to ending the war. The South did not have enough manpower to continue the fight without them. And enslaved people were willing to fight for their freedom. Robert Smalls's story was proof of that! So on January 1, 1863, Abraham Lincoln issued the Emancipation Proclamation. (A proclamation is a written statement of something important. Emancipation means being set free.) The Emancipation Proclamation freed all of the enslaved people in the Confederacy. After that, nearly two hundred thousand Black men joined the Union forces.

Abraham Lincoln

In April of 1865, the war ended with a Northern victory. The Confederate states had to return to the Union. Most important of all, slavery in the United States was over.

Many Southern cities, as well as farms, bridges, and railroad lines, had been destroyed during the fighting. And four million newly freed people needed a chance at a better life. The hard work of reuniting the country and rebuilding the South was about to begin.

CHAPTER 2
Lincoln's Plan

A year and a half before the Civil War ended, President Lincoln was already planning how to rebuild the nation. He wanted to repair, not punish, the rebel states. His plan said Confederate states could rejoin the United States if at least ten percent of voters in that state swore loyalty to the Union. Only then could they vote in elections and send members to the US Congress.

Having representation in Congress would once again make them full participants in the running of the nation.

In exchange, the Union would return all the property taken from Southerners during the war except, of course, for formerly enslaved people. Lincoln's plan became known as the Ten Percent Plan.

Was the president's plan too forgiving? Many thought so. After all, the rebel states had left the Union and started a war that killed hundreds of thousands of people on both sides.

The unfinished Capitol building in 1861, where both the Senate and House of Representatives meet

In Congress, some members of the Republican Party put together a much stricter plan for Reconstruction. They were known as Radical Republicans. *Radical* meant that they wanted big changes in the way the country was run. The group in Congress was led by Massachusetts senator Charles Sumner and Pennsylvania representative Thaddeus Stevens.

Branches of Government

The United States government is divided into three branches: executive, judicial, and legislative. Each branch has different powers. They work together so that no single branch has too much control.

The executive branch refers to the president and the president's advisors. The president is head of the military; deals with foreign countries; and in a yearly speech before Congress, goes over the important issues for the government to handle. The president cannot make laws but can veto, or turn down, proposed laws.

The legislative branch, also known as Congress, makes laws, oversees public money, and has the power to declare war. Congress is made up of the Senate and the House of Representatives. Each state has two senators. Its number of representatives depends on how many people live in the state.

The judicial branch is the court system that decides when laws have been broken. The highest court is the Supreme Court, which has nine justices.

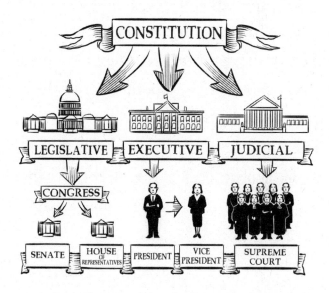

The federal government makes laws that apply to the nation as a whole. But each state is also allowed to make its own laws as long as they do not break any federal ones.

The Radical plan required a majority of voters in each former rebel state to swear loyalty to the Union. The plan also said that freedpeople must be treated equally under the law. (Freedpeople is another name for formerly enslaved people.)

Lincoln would not accept the Radical plan. He thought its terms would slow down the reunion of the country. Regardless of either plan, life for people in the South—both white and Black—was going to change.

The Southern economy was based on growing crops like tobacco, sugar, and cotton. In fact, selling cotton made so much money that it was called "King Cotton."

Before the Civil War, two groups ran this economy: a few rich white plantation owners and a great number of poor white farmers. Plantations were large farms that depended on enslaved labor. Enslaved people were worked to the breaking point under extremely cruel conditions and without pay.

The Emancipation Proclamation and a new law called the Thirteenth Amendment changed everything. Both said Black people in the Confederacy could no longer be enslaved. They were free.

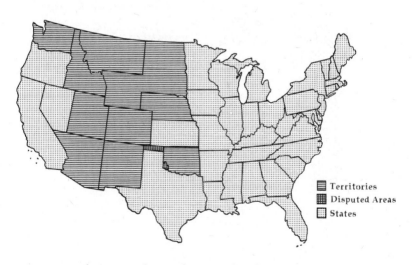

Territories
Disputed Areas
States

The reunited United States after the Civil War

Radical Leaders

At six feet, four inches, Charles Sumner (1811–1874) matched President Lincoln in height but outpaced him in his passion for equal rights. Before the war, Sumner was nearly beaten to death by a pro-slavery House member from South Carolina. Many Northerners were horrified by the attack. Radical abolitionists gained more support. And

Sumner was not to be swayed. Three years later, he returned to the Senate to continue to press for equality.

Charles Sumner

Thaddeus Stevens (1792–1868) was a craggy-faced man who firmly believed in freedom for all. He helped the Underground Railroad before the war. The Underground Railroad was a system of people who offered shelter and help to enslaved people escaping north. Stevens served in Congress until his death in 1868. He chose to be buried in a cemetery that accepted both races at a time when many graveyards were segregated. (*Segregated* means "separated by race.") His headstone explains his choice and mission in life, "Equality of Man Before His Creator."

Thaddeus Stevens

But what did freedom mean? How would the lives of Black people change? These were tough questions that Reconstruction would attempt to answer.

CHAPTER 3
A Blaze of Glory

As news of Emancipation swept through the South, all the newly freed people rejoiced. In Georgia, Houston H. Holloway described those first few days of his newfound freedom: "I felt like a bird out of a cage. Amen. Amen. Amen.

Houston H. Holloway

I could hardly ask to feel better than I did that day . . . The week passed off in a blaze of glory."

On February 18, 1865, Southerners of both races watched in awe as the Massachusetts Fifty-Fifth Regiment marched through the streets of

Charleston, South Carolina. These Northern soldiers were Black. White townspeople were outraged. But freedpeople welcomed the troops with parades, dancing, and singing. To them, the soldiers were heroes.

Now freedpeople were in charge of themselves. Long known only by the name of their slaveholder, many chose new last names. Choosing what to wear was another sign of freedom. The clothes enslaved people were given by their captors were often little better than rags. Black women and men alike began to wear bright, vibrant clothing with more elegant designs.

Once banned from large gatherings, African Americans now joined together to build their own communities. Freedpeople adopted children who could not find their parents. Churches and schools also provided a new sense of family. These places became centers of support and civil rights activism, a tradition that endures to this day.

Communities were coming together, but would that be enough? It had been the slaveholders' responsibility to feed, clothe, and house enslaved people. Many white people wondered if the freedpeople could do the same for themselves.

During the war, Union general William T. Sherman gave over four hundred thousand acres of plantation land directly to freedpeople in parts of the South. His orders became known as "forty acres and a mule," referring to giving land and a farm animal to freedpeople. Owning land could give Black people a chance to grow food

for themselves and sell food to others. Radical Republicans approved. Unfortunately, white Southerners did not. The plan only lasted a short while.

In March of 1865, the Freedmen's Bureau was set up to assist formerly enslaved people with housing and medical care. It also tried to arrange fair contracts for freedpeople who took jobs working for white landowners. As expected, many white Southerners were not happy with the new protections given freedpeople and ignored them. Some contracts even stated that everything should be "the same as in slavery time." Black workers were told to call their bosses "master." And if they did not, they were often attacked by angry white Southerners.

If working conditions for freedpeople were barely better than slavery, what did it mean to be free? For many, the answer was family.

Besides finding fair work, newly freed Black people desperately wanted to be reunited with missing relatives. Enslaved families had often been split apart. Children, husbands, and wives were often sold and sent to new plantations, never to see their loved ones again. This was the reason Robert Smalls made his great escape. As one Freedmen's Bureau agent said, "Emancipation was incomplete until the families which had been dispersed by slavery were reunited."

Black-owned newspapers in the North and the South began running "Information Wanted" ads. On October 14, 1865, *The Colored Tennessean* was full of notices like the following:

"*INFORMATION is wanted of my two boys, James and Horace, one of whom was sold in Nashville and the other was sold in Rutherford County. I, myself, was sold in Nashville and sent to Alabama, by Wm. Boyd. I and my children belonged to David Moss . . .*"

Any information sent would be "thankfully received."

If lost family members were reunited, a second type of story might run, such as, "Separated for

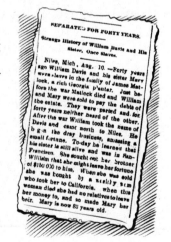

Forty Years. Strange History of William Davis and His Sister, Once Slaves."

On learning of his family's location, one man walked over six hundred miles to be with them again! A woman named Tempie Herndon Durham had been sold away from her husband. To her, freedom meant they could be together all of the time "stead of [just] Saturday an' Sunday."

Tempie Herndon Durham

Through employment, family, and community, freedpeople began to discover their independence. But the great African American civil rights leader and writer Frederick Douglass said what the formerly enslaved needed most was the vote. He believed that slavery would never really be over until "the Black man has the ballot." In other words, the right to vote. Only through voting would African Americans have a voice in government. They could elect people who would stand up for their needs.

Frederick Douglass

Up until this point in America's history, only white men were allowed to vote. No men of color and no women—white or Black—had the right to vote. This meant decisions affecting the whole country were made by less than 45 percent of the people in 1860. The idea of giving all Black men the right to vote was radical. Not even Abraham Lincoln believed in equal rights for all. But his opinions slowly changed.

In a speech after the war ended, Lincoln said he would consider giving some African Americans the right to vote.

John Wilkes Booth

Only two days later, on April 14, 1865, the president was shot and killed while attending the theater. His killer, John Wilkes Booth, was a Southerner. Wilkes believed in white supremacy, the misguided idea that white people are better than people of color.

Abraham Lincoln died before he could lead the nation through Reconstruction. So the job fell to his vice president, Andrew Johnson. On April 15, Johnson was sworn in as the seventeenth president of the United States. Would he be up to the task?

CHAPTER 4
New President, New Plan

"Whatever Andrew Johnson may be," Frederick Douglass once said, "he certainly is no friend of our race." Andrew Johnson was born in North Carolina in 1808. He grew up poor and hated wealthy Southern planters. But he also believed in white supremacy and supported slavery. In fact, Johnson had enslaved several people.

Andrew Johnson

After working his way out of poverty, Johnson became a senator in Tennessee. Tennessee was the last state to join the Confederacy. However, Johnson did not believe the Southern states had the right to leave the Union. In fact, he was the only Southern senator to remain in Congress once war broke out. Although he believed in white supremacy, Johnson eventually came to see emancipation as the way to end the war. For these reasons, Lincoln chose Johnson as his vice president when he ran for reelection in 1864.

GRAND NATIONAL UNION BANNER FOR 1864
LIBERTY, UNION AND VICTORY

Andrew Johnson being sworn in as president

When Johnson became president on April 15, 1865, Congress was not in session and would not return until December. (Congress members still take regular, but shorter breaks.)

This meant that for eight months, Johnson was completely in control of Reconstruction. Radical Republicans in Congress hoped Johnson's resentment of wealthy Southerners would lead to real improvements for Black people in the former Confederacy. Unfortunately, all Johnson wanted was to restore the rebel states to the Union as swiftly as possible. He had no interest in changing how those states governed themselves or treated Black Southerners.

In May 1865, Johnson put forth a plan similar to Lincoln's Ten Percent Plan. It gave amnesty to almost any former rebel willing to pledge loyalty to the Union. (The wealthiest landowners, however, had to ask for a presidential pardon.) Johnson's plan also assigned a temporary governor to each ex-Confederate state. These governors would make sure new state constitutions were written that met three requirements: The state needed to acknowledge the Thirteenth Amendment ending slavery. It also had to swear to never leave the Union again. Lastly, the Confederate government had created its own money. When it lost the war, that money became worthless. As a result, anyone who had done business with the Confederacy and been promised payment in Confederate dollars now needed to be paid in US currency. Owing money is also called debt. Johnson required each state to pay its own war debt.

Confederate money

While Johnson's plan was similar to Lincoln's in some ways, he also included protections for white supremacy. Johnson said only the people who held voting rights *before* the war could still vote. This meant only white men. No African Americans would be allowed to vote. Radical Republicans were furious. But Congress wasn't in session, so there was nothing they could do.

That spring, Johnson pardoned 7,197 wealthy former Confederates. He would go on to pardon over 6,000 more. Many of the rebel states had indeed formed new governments, but in reality very little had changed. In every rebel state, old Confederate leaders were still in charge. Confederate generals were elected to Congress.

Even Alexander Stephens, the vice president of the Confederate States, was elected to the US Senate. To make matters worse, these newly elected politicians had begun creating laws known as Black Codes.

Alexander Stephens

Black Codes existed in both the North and South. These laws sharply controlled the lives of African Americans. In the South, the codes made sure African Americans suffered under almost the same conditions they had during slavery. There, laws restricted education and where Black people could live. Some laws even prevented African Americans from owning dogs or guns.

African Americans needed to travel freely in order to find better jobs. Yet the Black Codes prevented this by limiting where and how far they could travel. If a Black person was spotted looking for work or gathering with others, they could be arrested for vagrancy. (A vagrant is a person who wanders from place to place without a home or a job.) If that happened, they could be thrown into prison or charged a large fine. If they could not pay the fine, they could then be forced to work for free until the phony debt was paid off.

Carpetbaggers and Scalawags

After the war, many Northerners, both Black and white, saw the defeated South as a land of opportunity. Some wanted to help rebuild or help freedpeople. But others hoped to make a quick dollar buying up farmland where plantations once stood. Whatever their reason for heading south, these Northerners were called "carpetbaggers." The nickname was not a compliment. It came from a style of suitcase made from a rug that many of these men carried.

White Southerners resented these Northern newcomers—particularly the Black Northerners who were educated and had been born free. They feared these carpetbaggers would teach freedpeople to stand up for themselves. But they had even more disdain for certain Southern folks whom they called scalawags. A scalawag was a Southern-born white person who supported giving more rights to Black people. Former Confederates saw them as traitors. To white supremacists, both carpetbaggers and scalawags were a threat to the old order of the South.

Black Codes also allowed white Southerners
to place African American children into
"apprenticeships." An apprenticeship is meant

to teach someone a skilled trade, such as shoe-making or carpentry. But in reality, these so-called "apprenticeships" forced children into unpaid slave labor. While some of these children were considered orphans, others were actually taken away from their parents.

Other codes prevented interracial marriage, and segregated public spaces and transportation. In short, they made Black people second-class citizens.

Throughout 1865 and 1866, these codes spread across the Southern states. Their sheer unfairness grabbed the attention of Northern Republicans who tried to stop Black Codes in their tracks. But the codes remained in place in the South, in one form or another, for the next hundred years.

Chinese Immigrants During Reconstruction

As freedpeople left the plantations, white planters turned to a new source of labor—Chinese men. Chinese immigrants had helped build the railways that connected the country east to west. They also worked in Northern factories. Southern planters believed Chinese workers would be cheap labor who could be controlled without interference from the government. But the pay was too low and the treatment too poor to attract Chinese workers

for long. Instead, they set out to find a different role in Southern society.

Because of segregation, white stores did not want to serve Black customers. Being neither African American nor white, Chinese people discovered they could run businesses that filled this gap. In Mississippi and Arkansas, they found success running grocery stores in Black neighborhoods. This trend continued in the 1960s, when the Great Migration and civil rights movement changed the shape of the South.

CHAPTER 5
The Same Old South

On a warm day in December 1865, Congress reassembled in Washington, DC. A big crowd of curious onlookers gathered to watch new representatives from the former Confederate states arrive to take their seats. But Congress refused to accept them. Republicans were worried these ex-Confederates would not fairly represent all the residents of the Southern states—especially not African Americans.

That afternoon, President Johnson gave a speech in which he declared that "Restoration" was complete. (Restoration was his term for Reconstruction.) The rebel states had met his simple requirements to rejoin the Union. The final step was for Congress to welcome the

Southern politicians. Johnson thought any other changes in law should be made by the states and not by the federal government. If freedpeople were patient, he told the gathering, white

Southerners would eventually reward them with the right to vote. But the evidence said otherwise.

One report from the South said, "The hatred toward the negro as a freeman is intense . . . Murders, shootings, whippings, robbing, and brutal treatment of every kind are daily inflicted upon them, and, I am sorry to say, in most cases

they can get no redress." (*Redress* means remedy or compensation.)

Not long after the president's speech, Senator Charles Sumner gave one of his own. He said it was his "duty to expose the actual condition of the rebel states, especially as regards loyalty and the treatment of the freemen."

He produced several reports describing the horrific abuse of Black Southerners. Some described Black men being tied to trees, or "strung up by the thumbs in the public square" and attacked by the same white lawmen who were supposed to protect them. Others mentioned "Regulators" who claimed to keep the peace by killing African Americans and harming any white people who treated them fairly.

The Radical Republicans in Congress had to move swiftly to prevent what they feared would simply be a new Confederacy. In January 1866, Congress put forth two bills. One would keep the Freedmen's Bureau open longer than planned and expand its authority. But most importantly, the second was the nation's first civil rights bill. It gave citizenship to anyone born in the United States. As citizens, freedpeople were automatically protected by the same laws as white Americans.

This was progress. But would it be enough?

On February 7, 1866, a group of African Americans met with President Johnson to make a case for citizenship and the right to vote. Among them was Frederick Douglass. The group believed freedmen should band together with poor white people in seeking true equality as Americans.

But President Johnson didn't believe freedmen and poor white people had anything in common.

He insisted that states should decide their own laws—including who could vote. When the civil rights and Freedmen's Bureau bills came to him for approval that March, he vetoed them both.

Those vetoes were like the first shots fired in a new war, this one between the president and Republicans in Congress. It was increasingly clear that neither the Southern states nor President Johnson had any intention of protecting the lives of African Americans.

Congress, however, has some power to work around a president. If two-thirds of Congress vote for an act after it has been vetoed, the president cannot veto it again. And that's exactly what happened. That April, radical and moderate

Republicans came together to pass the Civil Rights Act of 1866—without the president's

approval. From now on, almost anyone born in the United States would be considered a citizen regardless of race.

CHAPTER 6
The First Americans

Did the Civil Rights Act of 1866 protect all people in the United States? Unfortunately, no. It did not apply to Native Americans. During the Civil War, Native American tribes were considered their own nations, independent of the United States. That changed during Reconstruction, especially in the American South for the people whom white Americans called the "Five Civilized Tribes." The term *civilized* was insulting as it had nothing to do with the tribes' own rich culture. Instead, white people used it as a sign of approval for those tribes that had adapted to white American culture, language, and clothing. But even those changes did not protect their civil rights.

The Cherokee, Choctaw, Chickasaw, Muscogee-Creek, and Seminole nations had been forced to move west in the 1830s to what was called "Indian Territory." The forced migration became known as the Trail of Tears. Thousands of people perished on the journey.

Some Native Americans became slaveholders while others supported abolition. When the war began, several tribes made treaties with the Confederate states that were their closest neighbors. That meant tribes that remained loyal to the Union were suddenly surrounded by Confederate enemies. "Now the wolf has come . . . ," Creek leaders wrote to President Lincoln in 1861, "white people are trying to take our people away to fight against us and you."

Native American Union soldier

Their request for help was not answered. The Civil War devastated many tribes and the land on which they lived.

In 1866, the US government formed Reconstruction treaties with each of the "Five Civilized Tribes." The treaties required them to abolish slavery and give freedpeople citizenship as members of one of the nations. Some freedpeople chose to remain living in Native territory. Others left to seek their own fortunes. The fate of Native Americans themselves was also in question. The US government took away large areas of land that it had once agreed would belong to the tribes forever. Soon railways crisscrossed Indian Territory, bringing more white people to native lands.

In 1871, Congress passed an act that said Native American tribes were no longer their own nations. The people were now wards of the state. Wards are dependent on an authority figure. Native Americans who had proudly ruled themselves for hundreds of generations would now be ruled by a government in which they had no voice.

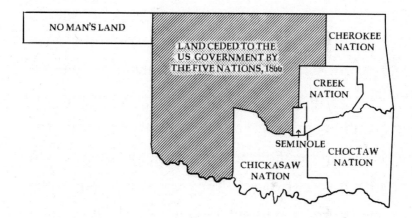

CHAPTER 7
The Fight for Freedom

In late April 1866, the committee on Reconstruction in Congress made its report. The former rebel states were disobeying the requirements that had let them return to the Union. Several of the new Southern congressmen still had not sworn the oath of loyalty. The committee suggested Congress not allow high ranking ex-Confederates to hold office. Nor should it welcome back any state that failed to protect the civil rights of all citizens.

White supremacists were working hard to take freedpeople's rights away. But Black Southerners had already begun using their civil rights to improve their lives. They were farming their own land and building churches

and schools in thriving communities.

This progress was met by terrible violence in May of 1866, in the city of Memphis, Tennessee. As one Northern newspaper reported, "The freedmen at Memphis . . . have been hunted in the streets, women and children shot in cold blood, their homes burnt over their heads . . . their churches and schools burnt to the ground."

By the end of the three-day massacre, scores of Black churches, schoolhouses, homes, and businesses had been destroyed. Forty-eight people lay dead. All but two were African American.

Many Northerners insisted Congress do more to protect Black citizens. So two months later, Congressional lawmakers passed the Fourteenth Amendment to the Constitution. It restated and supported the Civil Rights Act requirements for citizenship. It also encouraged Southern states to give Black men the right to vote.

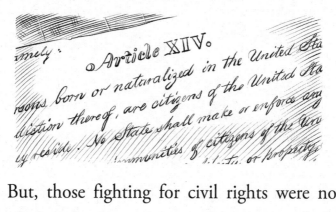

But, those fighting for civil rights were not satisfied with this new amendment. It still did not *guarantee* voting rights for Black men. And it completely blocked women from voting at all! Congress had to do more.

On July 16, Congress passed a new version of the Freedmen's Bureau bill to continue lending support to freedpeople in the South. Soon afterward, Tennessee became the first rebel state to ratify the Fourteenth Amendment and meet all of the requirements of readmission to the Union. Progress was being made.

Then on July 30, thirty-four African Americans and three white Republicans were killed in a wave of white supremacist violence in New Orleans, Louisiana. Similar scenes played out across the South and even in several Northern states throughout Reconstruction. But President Johnson continued to insist that his plan for "Restoration" was a success. He just needed to show Congress that the public agreed with him.

So he came up with an idea . . . that totally backfired.

At the end of August 1866, President Johnson began a tour of the country by train. He was usually a strong public speaker, but this time Johnson's speeches failed to win people over. Instead, they helped Radical Republicans gain more support in the November 1866 elections.

Meanwhile, people of diverse backgrounds continued to come together to learn about politics and their civil rights. A North Carolina freedmen's convention in October 1866 helped people to form local and statewide groups. These groups would spread the word about the suffering and rights of African Americans. Despite the violence, there was hope that the new laws would make life better for African Americans. A similar convention in

Alabama issued a statement declaring, "The law no longer knows white nor Black, but simply men."

More Black citizens were putting their trust in the law. It was time for Congress to prove that trust was well-placed. When the new Congress returned in 1867, Radical Republicans had enough control to push forward their own plan for Reconstruction with or without the president's help.

Women During Reconstruction

Reconstruction marked a change in the lives of women on both sides of the color line. Now, freedwomen could care for their own families without fear that their children might be sold off. Wealthy white Southern women had to learn how to raise their children and run a household without the help of enslaved servants. With many of their husbands killed in the war, these women also had to run farms or plantations on their own.

When the possibility of Black male suffrage arose, women's rights activists nationwide, such as Elizabeth Cady Stanton and Susan B. Anthony, hoped women would get the vote as well.

Elizabeth Cady Stanton and Susan B. Anthony

Instead, the Fourteenth Amendment made it clear that voting was for men and men alone, regardless of race. Women would not gain the right to vote nationwide until the Nineteenth Amendment was ratified in 1920.

CHAPTER 8
Radical Reconstruction

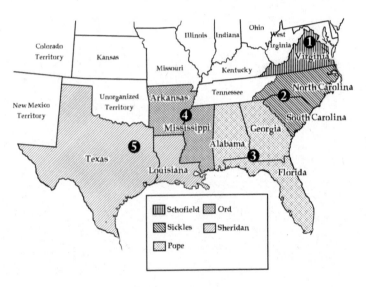

The Five Military Districts

The year 1867 marked the dawn of what is known as Radical Reconstruction. In March, Congress passed the Reconstruction Act of 1867. It went farther in guaranteeing rights for the newly freed. It also divided the South into five military districts under the control of Union soldiers. They were there to protect freedpeople. New state governments had to be created based on *universal* male suffrage. This meant that men of all races would be allowed to vote. The act also required the rebel states to approve the Fourteenth Amendment. President Johnson tried to veto it, but again Congress had enough power to overrule him.

For the first time, Black Americans could go to court if a crime had been committed against them. They could also serve on juries and travel where they pleased. Some states even began allowing Black men to vote—but it still wasn't a national law.

In the end, four Reconstruction Acts were passed. And they had the desired effect. By midyear, Southern Black men began to register to vote in the November elections. Voting allowed them to choose leaders who could represent the causes of freedpeople. At long last, their voices would be heard! By the following year, more than 80 percent of eligible African American men would be registered to vote.

Over the course of Reconstruction, sixteen African Americans were elected to Congress, including Robert Smalls. In all, five of them were formerly enslaved. Hundreds more Black men were elected to state and local positions as legislators, sheriffs, mayors, and judges. A few short years after slavery ended, the United States government was finally becoming more inclusive!

Blanche K. Bruce, Joseph H. Rainey, and Josiah Walls

Hiram R. Revels

Hiram R. Revels was the first African American US senator. Revels was a preacher who had been born free in North Carolina. He was elected to the US Senate in 1870. When Revels reported to Congress that February, Southern Democrats refused to let him take his seat in the Senate chamber. It took three days and an impassioned speech by Senator Charles Sumner before Revels was officially recognized.

In 1870, Joseph H. Rainey became the first African American to serve as a member of the House of Representatives. He was also the first formerly enslaved person in Congress. Rainey's father had purchased his family's freedom when Rainey was young. Elected in South Carolina in 1870, Rainey would go on to serve for more than eight years. He became the longest serving Black congressman of his day.

Joseph H. Rainey

President Johnson was furious at Congress for passing the Reconstruction Acts without his approval. He decided to make his own move.

As president, Johnson was the commander in chief of the military. He believed this gave him the power to replace his own advisors, called the cabinet. He wanted to replace the secretary of war, a supporter of Radical Reconstruction named Edwin Stanton. The

Edwin Stanton

president didn't have the power to do this. But he was stubborn, and in February of 1868, he fired Stanton anyway.

That was all it took for Congress to act. *Johnson* was the one who should be fired! In February 1868, the US House of Representatives moved to impeach the president.

Impeachment is a process by which Congress can charge a public official—even the president—of a crime or bad conduct. Johnson became the first US president to be impeached in the history of the nation. His Senate trial lasted from March until May in 1868. At stake was the presidency itself.

Some people were afraid of what impeachment

might mean for the government. It was a drastic move, to force out a president. Would impeachment become common in the future?

Andrew Johnson's impeachment trial

If the impeachment succeeded, Johnson would be forced to leave office. Because Johnson had replaced Abraham Lincoln after his tragic death, Johnson did not have a vice president. The next person in line for the presidency was Ohio senator Benjamin Wade. Wade was an important Radical Republican. President Johnson

Benjamin Wade

was not well liked in the Senate, but not everyone wanted his replacement to be a Radical president. Fifty-four senators voted. It would take a two-thirds majority— or thirty-six "guilty" votes— to throw Johnson out of office. Would they get enough?

When the trial ended, thirty-five senators voted "guilty" and nineteen did not. President Johnson was declared not guilty by a single vote!

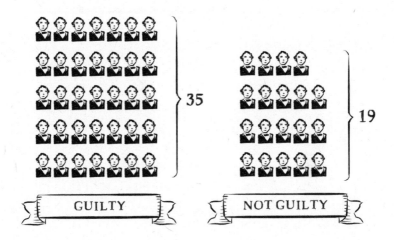

GUILTY } 35   NOT GUILTY } 19

He would remain president until the end of his term. And he would continue to interfere with Reconstruction.

On the Fourth of July, President Johnson, headstrong as ever, issued a blanket pardon to all ex-Confederates except for those who had been charged with treason or other crimes. By mid-July, Alabama, Arkansas, Florida, Louisiana, North Carolina, and South Carolina had been readmitted to the Union. The last state in the former Confederacy, Georgia, would not be readmitted until 1870.

Former Confederate states and the year
they were readmitted to the Union

Now all eyes turned to the presidential election of 1868. Johnson simply didn't have enough support to win. The Union war hero, General Ulysses S. Grant, was about to take the stage.

Grant was a popular figure among freedpeople and Union loyalists. He accepted the nomination of the Republican Party in May 1868 with the words, "Let us have peace." This became his campaign slogan. It appealed to Americans of all races who were tired of conflict and violence. Thanks in part to overwhelming support from new Black voters and white Southern Republicans, Grant became the eighteenth president of the United States.

Grant promised to continue Reconstruction. But between the failed impeachment trial that spring and the death of Congressman Thaddeus Stevens, public support for Radical Reconstruction was beginning to fade. On January 1, 1869, the Freedmen's Bureau closed down most of its operation. And violence against Black people continued to rise in a movement known as Redemption.

CHAPTER 9
The Rise of Redemption

Redemption means saving someone, or yourself, from mistakes or bad behavior. Normally, it has a positive meaning. But during Reconstruction, Redemption meant bringing the South back to the days of slavery as much as possible. Supporters of Redemption were called Redeemers. They used violence and intimidation, or fear, to strip away the newly won rights of freedpeople.

One of the worst incidents of violence was the Opelousas Massacre of 1868. On September 28, angry Democrats burst into a Black schoolhouse in Opelousas, Louisiana. They beat the teacher, a white "carpetbagger" from Ohio who was also a Republican newspaper editor. The students fled and told their families of the attack. A small group of Black people went to the rescue, fearing the teacher had been killed. (He had actually managed to escape.) At the sight of the rescue party, white residents went running for their guns. Over the course of two weeks, an estimated 250 men, women, and children were killed. Most of them were Black.

That fall, not a single vote for the Republican presidential candidate Ulysses S. Grant was cast in Opelousas. Why? Because Black Southerners and white Republicans feared they would pay for suffrage with their lives.

In order to guarantee universal voting rights for all Black men, Congress had to pass yet another law—the Fifteenth Amendment. Even so, in the South, few Black people felt safe enough to vote. And with good reason. That November, Tennessee became the first ex–rebel state to be "redeemed" by electing a Democrat-controlled, all-white state government. Southern white Democrats remained in power there for the next hundred years.

Violent white supremacy groups were growing bigger and becoming more organized. The most well-known of these was the Ku Klux Klan.

The Klan, or KKK, first appeared in Tennessee around 1865 or 1866. It was a secret organization

created by ex-Confederate soldiers and led by former general Nathan Bedford Forrest. The name Ku Klux Klan comes from the Greek word for "circle" and the Scottish word "clan," which refers to a close-knit group or family. Thousands

of African Americans and white Republicans were
murdered during Reconstruction and beyond
by white supremacist groups like the Klan.

In 1870, Congress held a series of hearings
on the Ku Klux Klan in which victims and

witnesses testified to the Klan's acts of terror. On May 31, 1870, Congress passed the first of three Enforcement Acts in an attempt to stop the Klan. The first act made interfering with voting rights a federal crime. The second Enforcement Act passed in February 1871. It allowed federal officials to oversee voter registration. This was meant to protect Black voters from white terrorists at the polls. Two months later, Congress passed what became known as the Ku Klux Klan Act. It authorized President Grant to use the military to enforce that protection.

Did any of this help? Unfortunately, not much. Violence against African Americans continued to spread, and not just in the South. In October 1871, in the northern city of Philadelphia, Pennsylvania, three African Americans were killed when they showed up to vote.

Less than a week later, Klan terrorism in South Carolina reached a boiling point. Using the powers given him by the new Ku Klux Klan Act, Grant sent the army in to protect the peace in Southern states. Thanks in part to the large presence of soldiers, by the end of 1871 the Klan was for the most part dismantled.

But other white supremacist groups rose up to take its place. The Klan would eventually resurface in the next century.

The rest of the country was growing tired of the focus on Reconstruction. People felt there were other problems that needed to be solved. The government help that had poured forth in those first few years of Radical Reconstruction was coming to an end.

CHAPTER 10
Dark Days

In May of 1872, Congress debated passing an amnesty act. The new law would allow more than a hundred thousand Confederate veterans to reenter politics. What kind of effect would this have in Southern states that were starting to elect Black politicians?

Jefferson Long was the first Black representative from Georgia. Worried about the flood of ex-Confederate voters, he became the first African American to speak before the House of Representatives. He said, "As a man raised a slave, my mother a slave before me, and my ancestry slaves as far back as I can trace them . . . I venture to prophesy you will again have trouble from the very same men who gave you trouble before."

Jefferson Long speaks to Congress

He knew that allowing so many ex-rebels to vote and run for office would seriously damage Republican Reconstruction. Unfortunately, Congress ignored his warning. The Amnesty Act passed and sure enough the ranks of the Democratic Party swelled.

The following month, Congress voted to close the Freedmen's Bureau permanently. The bureau had never been perfect—there had never been enough people working for it. Yet it had tried to protect the newly emancipated. Now, even that protection was gone, as became clear the following April in 1873, with the horrific Colfax Massacre.

In Colfax, Louisiana, both Democrats and Republicans claimed to have won the local elections for sheriff and judge. Worried that anti-Reconstruction Democrats would take over the local government, a group of Black Republicans attempted to protect the courthouse. A large mob of white men responded with guns and a cannon.

They set fire to the courthouse. More than one hundred African Americans were murdered.

That same month, the US Supreme Court decided in favor of the Slaughterhouse Cases. The cases involved the rights of butchers, but their real importance was more wide reaching. The Supreme Court decision said it was the responsibility of state governments—not the federal government—to protect people's civil rights. This dealt a heavy blow to the freedom of African Americans in Southern states where Redeemer governments were in control.

That fall, the country's economy took a downturn. Northerners were more concerned with losing their jobs and homes than with the ongoing troubles of the South. The following year, the Freedman's Savings and Trust bank went bust. The savings of tens of thousands of

The Freedman's Savings and Trust bank

African Americans were lost in the blink of an eye. Reconstruction was falling apart. But it was the fall midterm elections that landed the biggest blow. (US midterm elections are when voters choose Congressional members but not a president.)

For the first time since the Civil War, Democrats won the House of Representatives. Republicans no longer held the majority in both houses of Congress. The outgoing Republican House passed more acts to prevent the segregation of public places and transportation. But these federal laws would not be enough to protect the rights of Black citizens from the white supremacists now in control of Southern states.

By the fall of 1876, only three Southern states remained in Republican control: Louisiana, South Carolina, and Florida. In South Carolina, the Democratic nominee for governor was a former Confederate general named Wade Hampton.

Wade Hampton

His supporters were called "Red Shirts" because of their uniforms. They began a campaign of terror against Black and Republican voters. As one writer later said, Red Shirts were "honor bound to control [or stop] the vote of at least one negro, by intimidation . . ." and even murder. The election results were in dispute for months. Ultimately, despite clear signs of cheating, Hampton remained in office. South Carolina became a Redeemer state.

The presidential election that year was a circus. Republican Rutherford B. Hayes ran against Democrat Samuel Tilden for president.

Rutherford B. Hayes

Samuel Tilden

Hayes supported rights for African Americans. But Black Southerners were again kept from the polls by Redeemers. To make matters worse, Democrats illegally cast multiple votes. In the end, the race was so close that both candidates claimed victory.

In Congress, Republicans realized that they

would have to make a deal with Southern Democrats in order for Hayes to become president. Secret meetings were held without any Black congressmen present. A terrible agreement was made. In exchange for Southern votes and the presidency, Hayes would end Reconstruction once and for all. This was politics and not democracy at work. "To such a bargain," African American Congressman John R. Lynch later wrote, "I did not care to be even an innocent party."

On March 4, 1877, Rutherford B. Hayes became president. By his order, the military pulled its remaining troops out of the South. Reconstruction was over. Redemption had won.

CHAPTER 11
Legacy

The painful legacy of Reconstruction can be found in the spread of more Black Codes, also known as Jim Crow laws, that oppressed African Americans in the South for the next hundred years. Despite continual efforts by some to end segregation, voter intimidation, and terror, it wasn't until the sweeping civil rights movements of the 1950s and '60s that radical change occurred.

For many decades, white supremacist beliefs and organizations continued to spread violence through the South. In murder trials, even when the white killers of Black people were known, they were not punished. Some of these organizations still exist to this day.

These conditions gave rise to the Exoduster

movement in 1879. An exodus is a departure. Exodusters were freedpeople who left the South to settle in midwestern states such as Kansas.

Life was not much easier there, however. In the early 1900s, a much bigger exodus began that lasted until the 1970s. It was called the Great Migration. Millions of African Americans left the South seeking a better life in northern cities such as Detroit, Chicago, and New York, and also out west in California. At the start of the Great

Migration, 90 percent of Black people lived in the South. By the end, 47 percent had moved north or west. All were escaping the failed promises of Reconstruction.

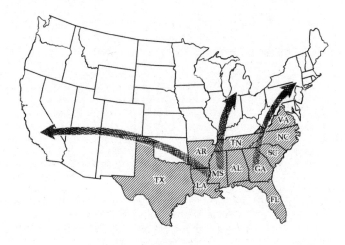

The arrows show where people went during the Great Migration.

For many years, white historians, led by a man named William Dunning, tried to blame Reconstruction's failure on African Americans. Dunning refused to believe Black people could be responsible citizens. In 1915, the release of a movie called *Birth of a Nation* solidified this belief in many American minds. The movie tells the story of a Northern and Southern family during Reconstruction. It is well known for its racist depictions of African Americans and its glorification of the Klan.

Twenty years later, famous African American writer, historian, and speaker W.E.B. Du Bois published a book called *Black Reconstruction in America*. The book collected the unheard stories and experiences of African Americans during Reconstruction. It showed how wrong Dunning was, and proved how hard freedpeople had worked  to improve their lives. Du Bois's book eventually led to a reexamination of the Reconstruction era.

Today, it is agreed that Reconstruction was not destined to fail. The era marks one of the greatest periods of hope in American history. But the promise of Reconstruction was never fully realized. It wasn't until the 1960s that the United States again guaranteed civil rights and voting rights through acts of Congress. Even today, African Americans still struggle for equality in the eyes of the law and their fellow citizens.

In the early twentieth century, the Republican and Democratic parties began to change. Democrats grew more concerned with social change while Republicans became more conservative. (Both the first African American president, Barack Obama, and the first African

Barack Obama

Kamala Harris

American and Indian American female vice president, Kamala Harris, are Democrats.) Despite this change in the two parties, history seems to be repeating itself.

In 2020, the Republican party began working to restrict voting. As of 2021, nineteen states had passed new laws that some say will make it harder for Americans—especially people of color—to vote. At the same time, Democrats in Congress worked to introduce new voter protections with the Freedom to Vote Act and John Lewis Voting Rights Advancement Act.

In some ways the work of Reconstruction continues to this day. Hopefully the progress made for a few brief years in the late 1860s and '70s can also serve as an inspiration for what may ultimately be achieved—a true democracy where all people are treated as equals.

Timeline of Reconstruction

1863	Abraham Lincoln signs the Emancipation Proclamation
Jan 1865	Congress approves the Thirteenth Amendment, abolishing slavery
Mar 1865	The Bureau of Refugees, Freedmen, and Abandoned Lands is created
Apr 1865	The Civil War ends with a Union victory
	President Lincoln is murdered
May 1865	President Andrew Johnson announces Reconstruction
Dec 1865	President Johnson declares Reconstruction complete
Apr 1866	Congress passes first civil rights bill
May 1866	Forty-eight African Americans killed by white Southerners in Memphis, Tennessee
July 1868	The Fourteenth Amendment is ratified
Nov 1868	Ulysses S. Grant is elected president
1870	The Fifteenth Amendment is ratified
1873	Colfax Massacre occurs
1874	Robert Smalls is elected to US House of Representatives for South Carolina
1875	The Civil Rights Act of 1875 enacted
1877	Rutherford B. Hayes becomes president
	Reconstruction officially ends

Timeline of the World

1863 — In Switzerland, the Red Cross is established

1865 — British writer Lewis Carroll publishes *Alice's Adventures in Wonderland*

1867 — Canada gains independence from Britain

— The United States buys Alaska from Russia

1868 — American writer Louisa May Alcott publishes first part of *Little Women*

1869 — The first professional baseball team is formed in Cincinnati, Ohio, and wins every game that year

— The first transcontinental railway is completed

— Wyoming becomes the first US territory to give women the right to vote

1871 — The Great Chicago Fire destroys almost a third of the city

1872 — Yellowstone becomes the United States' first national park

1873 — Levi Strauss patents denim jeans in San Francisco

1876 — Alexander Graham Bell receives patent for his invention, the telephone

1877 — The ballet *Swan Lake* premieres in Moscow

— Thomas Edison invents the phonograph and makes the first recording of the human voice

Bibliography

*Books for young readers

*Barton, Chris, and Don Tate. *The Amazing Age of John Roy Lynch*. Grand Rapids, MI: Eerdmans Books for Young Readers, 2015.

Foner, Eric. *A Short History of Reconstruction: Updated Edition*. New York: Harper Perennial, 2015.

*Gates, Henry Louis, Jr. *Dark Sky Rising: Reconstruction and the Dawn of Jim Crow*. New York: Scholastic, 2019.

*Gill, Joel Christian. *Robert Smalls: Tales of the Talented Tenth, no. 3*. Chicago: Chicago Review Press, 2021.

Lineberry, Cate. *Be Free or Die: The Amazing Story of Robert Smalls' Escape from Slavery to Union Hero*. New York: St. Martin's Press, 2017.

Litwack, Leon F. *Been in the Storm So Long: The Aftermath of Slavery*. New York: Knopf, 1979.

Sterling, Dorothy, ed. *The Trouble They Seen: The Story of Reconstruction in the Words of African Americans*. New York: De Capo Press, 1994.

MPI/Archive Photos/Getty Images

Representative Robert Smalls

Corbis Historical/Getty Images

Black Union soldiers during the Civil War

Buyenlarge/Archive Photos/Getty Images

Black Union soldier, 1862

Kean Collection/Archive Photos/Getty Images

The Emancipation Proclamation

Senator Charles Sumner

Representative Thaddeus Stevens

H. Armstrong Roberts/ClassicStock/Archive Photos/Getty Images

The Massachusetts Fifty-Fifth Regiment marches through Charleston, South Carolina, 1865.

Corbis Historical/Getty Images

Students and teachers stand outside a school for freedpeople in South Carolina, 1865.

Bettmann/Getty Images

Writer and abolitionist Frederick Douglass

Universal Images Group/Getty Images

President Andrew Johnson

Carpetbag from the 1860s at the Metropolitan Museum of Art

Memphis Massacre of 1866

Photo 12/Universal Images Group/Getty Images

Harper's Weekly front page of Black men voting

Buyenlarge/Archive Photos/Getty Images

Senator Hiram R. Revels

Buyenlarge/Archive Photos/Getty Images

Representative Joseph H. Rainey

The impeachment trial for Andrew Johnson, 1868

Bettmann/Getty Images

Print Collector/Hulton Archive/Getty Images

General Ulysses S. Grant, later elected president

Library of Congress/Corbis Historical/Getty Images

HON. JEFFERSON F. LONG.

REPRESENTATIVE FROM GEORGIA.

ENGRAVED FOR BARNES HISTORY OF CONGRESS

Representative Jefferson Long

Bettmann/Getty Images

Author of *Black Reconstruction in America*, W.E.B. Du Bois